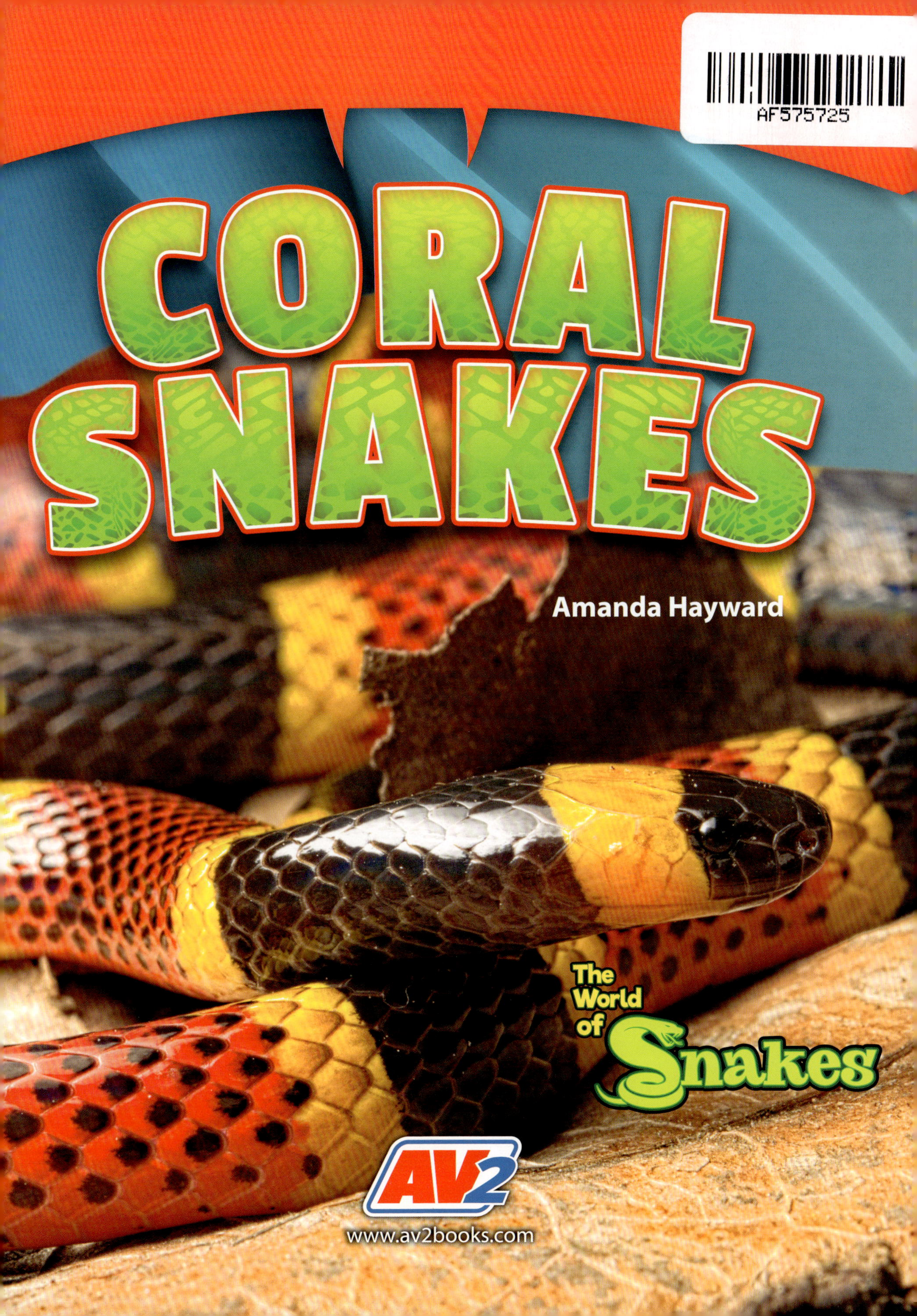
AF575725
CORAL SNAKES
Amanda Hayward
The World of Snakes
AV2
www.av2books.com

Step 1
Go to **www.av2books.com**

Step 2
Enter this unique code
VUHNJR1PL

Step 3
Explore your interactive eBook!

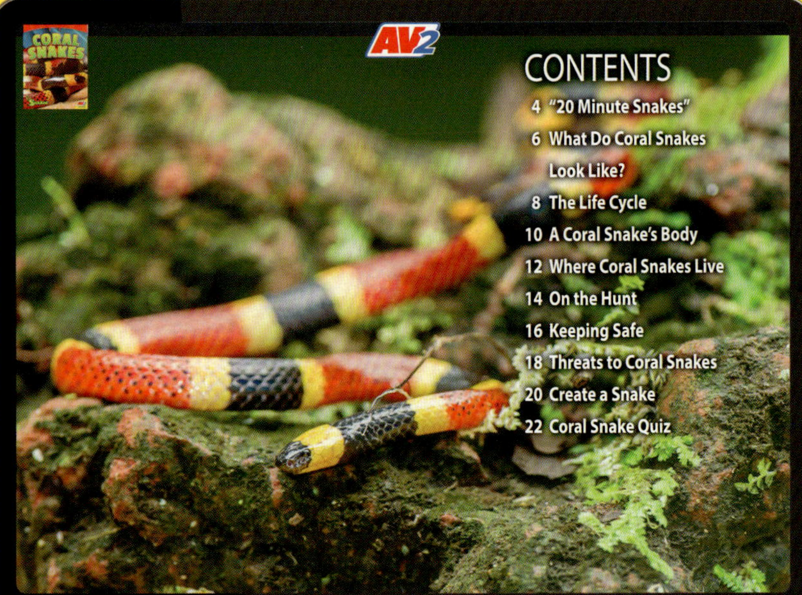

AV2 is optimized for use on any device

Your interactive eBook comes with...

Contents
Browse a live contents page to easily navigate through resources

Audio
Listen to sections of the book read aloud

Videos
Watch informative video clips

Weblinks
Gain additional information for research

Slideshows
View images and captions

Try This!
Complete activities and hands-on experiments

Key Words
Study vocabulary, and complete a matching word activity

Quizzes
Test your knowledge

Share
Share titles within your Learning Management System (LMS) or Library Circulation System

Citation
Create bibliographical references following the Chicago Manual of Style

This title is part of our AV2 digital subscription

1-Year 3–8 Subscription
ISBN 978-1-7911-3306-1

Access hundreds of AV2 titles with our digital subscription.
Sign up for a FREE trial at **www.av2books.com/trial**

CORAL SNAKES

CONTENTS

2 AV2 Book Code
4 "20 Minute Snakes"
6 What Do Coral Snakes Look Like?
8 The Life Cycle
10 A Coral Snake's Body
12 Where Coral Snakes Live
14 On the Hunt
16 Keeping Safe
18 Threats to Coral Snakes
20 Create a Snake
22 Coral Snake Quiz
23 Key Words/Index

"20 Minute Snakes"

Coral snakes, or corals, are known to be very dangerous snakes. In Mexico, these **venomous** snakes are known as "20 minute snakes." This is because a bite from one can kill a person very quickly. Coral snakes are part of the elapid family. Other snakes in this family include cobras, sea snakes, and mambas.

WARNING

Coral snakes have one of the **strongest** venoms of all known snakes. Their venom can cause the heart and lungs to stop working.

Coral snakes are reptiles. Like other reptiles, they have scaly skin and are cold-blooded. They use energy from the Sun to keep warm and the shade to keep cool.

SNAKE BITES

There are **more than 100** coral snake species.

The eastern coral snake, Texas coral snake, and the Arizona coral snake are the **only three** types of coral snakes in the United States.

What Do Coral Snakes Look Like?

Coral snakes are not considered to be big snakes. Many corals are as thin as a pencil. They average between 18 and 30 inches (46 and 76 centimeters) long. The largest corals only reach up to about 4 feet (1.2 meters) in length.

Measuring Up

Average snake lengths

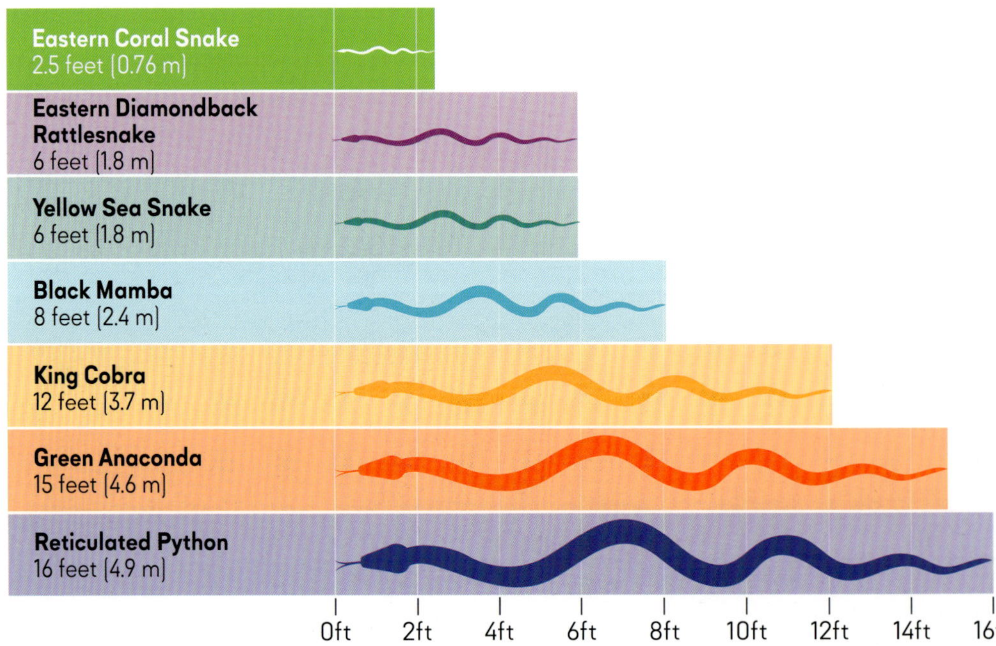

Coral snakes typically have brightly patterned scales. In the Americas, these snakes are often "coral" red with black, yellow, or white stripes. These stripes circle around their bellies.

Coral snakes in Asia can also be pink or blue. Some of these coral snakes do not have stripes. Instead, they may have solid colors.

The Life Cycle

Like all living things, coral snakes have a life cycle. A coral snake will be born, grow, and **reproduce**. Coral snakes in **captivity** can live 7 years or more.

1

Coral snakes are the only venomous snakes in North America that lay their eggs. A coral snake lays up to seven eggs.

2
Coral snake eggs hatch after 60 to 70 days. A baby coral snake is independent. It can survive on its own.
3
Young coral snakes spend much of their time hiding. As they grow, they shed their skin. Coral snakes are considered adults after about two years.
4
Because coral snakes often hide, people know little about how they find mates. North American coral snakes lay eggs during the summer.

A Coral Snake's Body

Like all living things, a coral snake has many different **adaptations**. Some keep the snake safe. Others help it to survive in its **habitat**.

Scales
A coral snake is covered by protective scales. They are made of keratin, the same material as human fingernails.

Tail
A coral snake's tail is often rounded. This makes it look like the snake's head.

Fangs

Coral snakes have short **fangs**. Unlike those of snakes such as rattlesnakes, coral snake fangs cannot fold up.

Tongue

Coral snakes use their tongues to sense the world around them. A snake's tongue helps it detect smells and feel vibrations.

Where Coral Snakes Live

Coral snakes can be divided into two different groups. These are Old World snakes and New World snakes. Old World snakes live in Asia. New World snakes live in North and South America. Coral snake habitats include forests, grasslands, rainforests, and wetlands.

Coral Snake Range

Asia

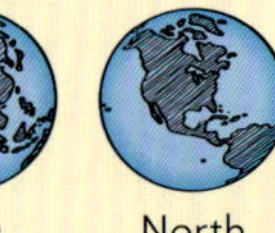
North America

South America

Coral Snake Habitats

Forest

Grassland

Rainforest

Wetland

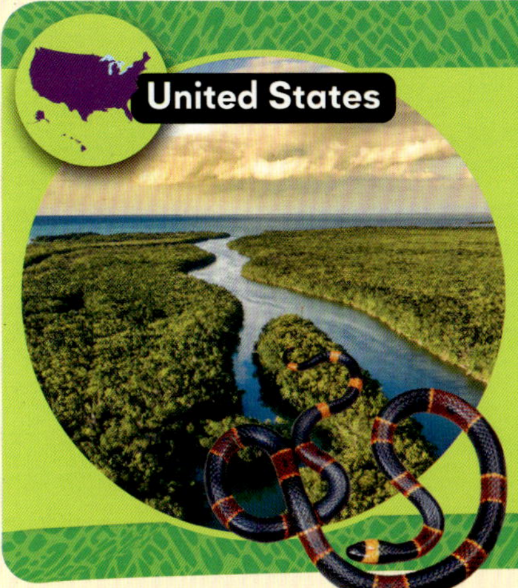

Eastern Coral Snake

Eastern coral snakes live in grasslands, forests, and wetlands. Their stripes follow a pattern where red touches yellow but not black. Some non-venomous snakes **mimic** these patterns. A rhyme was created to help tell them apart. "Red touching yellow, kill a fellow, red touching black, poisons lack."

Aquatic Coral Snake

Aquatic coral snakes are good swimmers. They spend most of their time in the water. Aquatic coral snakes are among the largest coral snakes. They eat eels, other fish, and some **amphibians**. These snakes are found in rainforest habitats in countries such as Brazil.

Blue Malayan Coral Snake

These snakes are found in the jungles of Southeast Asia, in countries such as Indonesia. Their venom is different than that of other corals. It causes instant **paralysis**. There is no **antivenin** for this type of bite.

On the Hunt

Many coral snakes are **nocturnal**. They sleep for most of the day. They hunt in the morning and early evening. Coral snakes have poor vision and no ears. They feel vibrations to search out **prey**. A coral's fangs are less than a quarter inch (6 millimeters) long. They often have to "chew" on their prey to inject their venom.

A coral snake may rest weeks before eating again after a large meal.

Coral snakes swallow their food whole. Their jaws can stretch to allow them to eat bigger food. Coral snakes eat insects, reptiles, fish, birds, and small **mammals**.

Coral snakes often eat small snakes. This sometimes includes eating other coral snakes.

Keeping Safe

Corals spend most of their time under ground. They hide under rocks and leaves. This helps them avoid coyotes, foxes, and birds of prey. Above ground, their bright colors act as a warning. They also scare **predators** away by releasing gas to make "popping" noises. Coral snakes usually bite only if they have no other options. About half of coral snake bites are "dry." This means that the snake bites without using any venom.

Coral snakes may use their tails as a distraction. A coral hides its head as its tail moves around. It pretends to attack anything that comes near.

Warning colors in animals such as coral snakes are known as aposematism. This word comes from Greek words meaning "away" and "sign."

Threats to Coral Snakes

Although deadly, coral snakes are not a major threat to people. They only bite when provoked. Humans are actually more of a threat to them.

Preserving coral snakes is important. They can be helpful to people. Scientists are studying coral snake venom. It might help people find new treatments for pain and diseases.

None of the three U.S. coral snake species are considered in danger globally, but some are threatened within certain states.

Across the world, snake numbers are decreasing. Loss of their habitat is thought to be the cause. As trees are cut down, snake homes are lost. Snakes, and the animals they eat, have no place to go. This puts some coral snakes at risk. Counting coral snake numbers is hard because they spend most of their lives hiding. However, several coral snake species, including the Roatan coral snake from Honduras, are either **endangered** or critically endangered.

Roatan coral snakes are only found on a single island.

SNAKE BITES

The Roatan coral snake was declared critically endangered **in 2010**.

Scientists believe that there are **more than 100,000** eastern coral snakes in the United States.

ACTIVITY
Create a Snake

There are many different kinds of snakes in the world. They all have certain features in common. However, each snake also has its own unique features. They help the snake live in its home.

Make your own snake by answering the following questions:

1. What is your snake called?
2. Where does it live?
3. What features does it share with other snakes?
4. What features help it live in its home? How do these features do this?
5. What does your snake look like?
6. Use a pencil or pen to draw your snake living in its home. Make sure to include all of its features.

Supplies needed for this activity

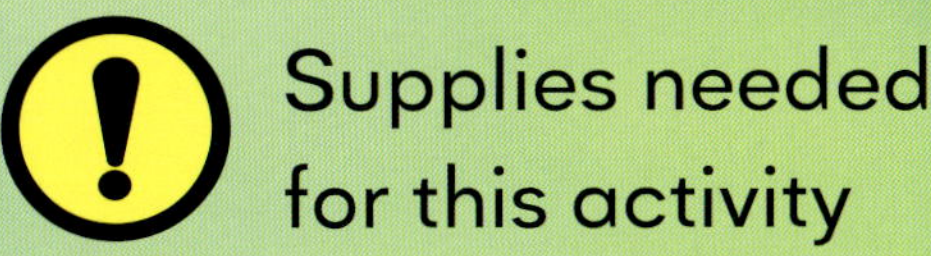

Eraser
Pencil or pen
Paper

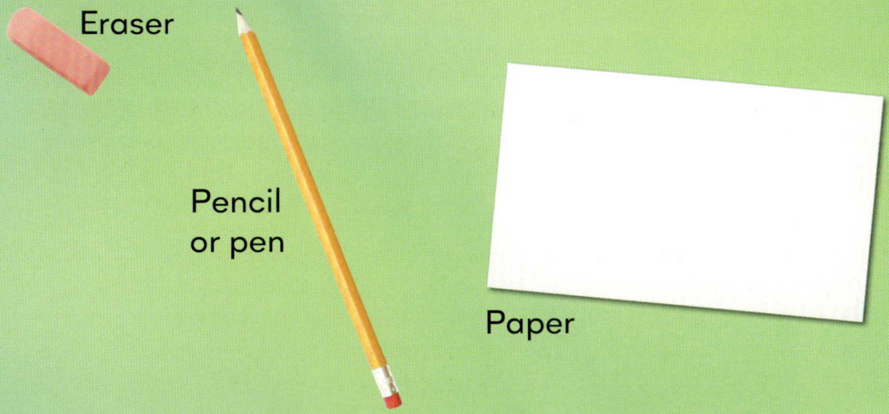

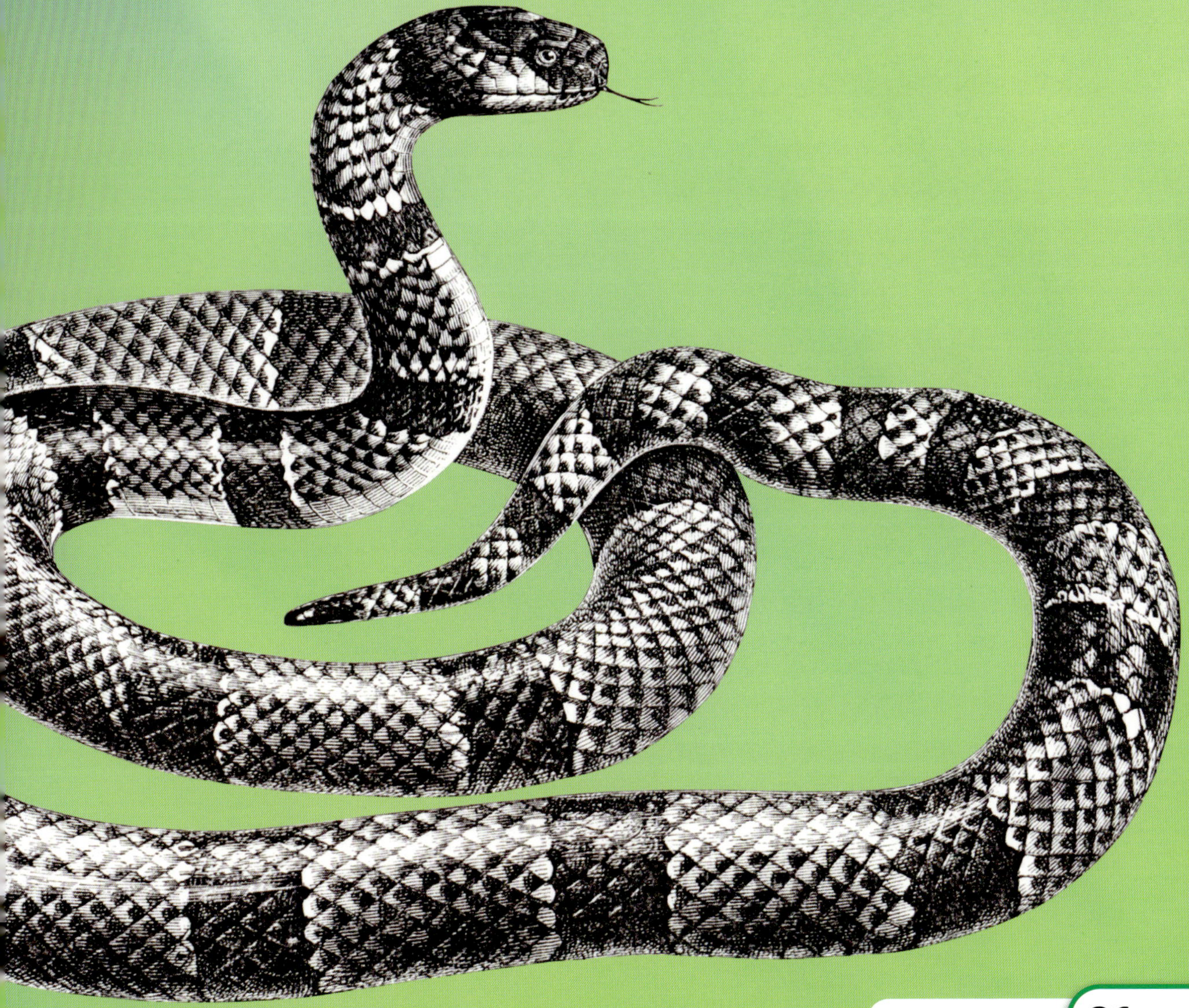

CORAL SNAKE QUIZ

How well do you know your coral snakes? Take this short quiz to find out.

1. Why are scientists studying coral snake venom?
2. What colors are on the body of an eastern coral snake?
3. On how many islands are Roatan coral snakes found?
4. How are baby coral snakes born?
5. When will a coral snake bite?
6. On which continents do coral snakes live?

7. What covers a coral snake's body?

8. How is the venom from a Blue Malayan coral snake unique?

ANSWERS

1. To find new cures for pain and diseases **2.** Red, yellow, and black
3. One **4.** They hatch from eggs **5.** When it has no other options
6. Asia, North America, and South America **7.** Scales **8.** It causes instant paralysis

Key Words

adaptations: changes in animals or plants that make them better able to survive in their homes

amphibians: cold-blooded animals that spend time in water

antivenin: medicine used to cure venom

captivity: an animal that is cared for by humans

endangered: a group of animals that are almost extinct

fangs: sharp, pointed teeth or similar parts of an animal's mouth

habitat: the place where a plant or animal lives

mammals: warm-blooded animals that are covered in hair

mimic: to copy or imitate

nocturnal: an animal that is active at night

paralysis: when an animal loses the ability to move its body

predators: animals that hunt other animals

prey: animals that are hunted by other animals

reproduce: to have babies

venomous: an animal or plant that produces toxic chemicals

aquatic coral snake 13
Arizona coral snake 5

Blue Malayan coral snake 13, 22
Brazil 12, 13

cobras 4, 6

eastern coral snake 5, 6, 13, 19, 22
eggs 8, 9, 22

fangs 11, 14

Indonesia 12, 13

mambas 4, 6
Mexico 4

reptiles 5, 15
Roatan coral snake 19, 22

skin 5, 9

Texas coral snake 5
tongue 11

United States 5, 12, 13, 19

venom 4, 13, 14, 16, 18, 22

Get the best of both worlds.

AV2 bridges the gap between print and digital.

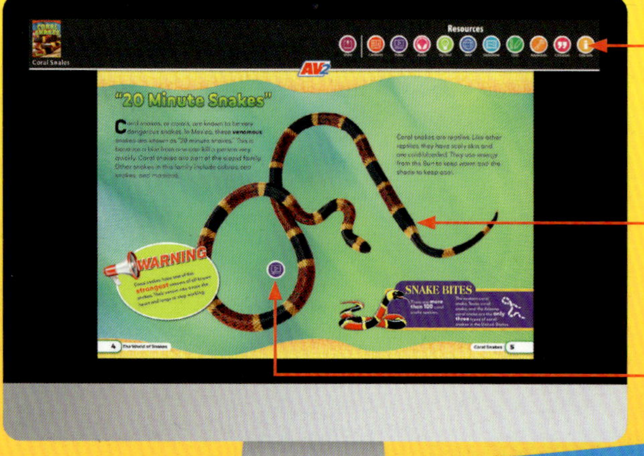

The expandable resources toolbar enables quick access to content including **videos**, **audio**, **activities**, **weblinks**, **slideshows**, **quizzes**, and **key words**.

Animated videos make static images come alive.

Resource icons on each page help readers to further **explore key concepts**.

Published by AV2
276 5th Avenue
Suite 704 #917
New York, NY 10001
Website: www.av2books.com

Library of Congress Control Number: 2021940109

ISBN 978-1-7911-4163-9 (hardcover)
ISBN 978-1-7911-4164-6 (softcover)
ISBN 978-1-7911-4165-3 (multi-user eBook)

Printed in Guangzhou, China
1 2 3 4 5 6 7 8 9 0 25 24 23 22 21

062021
101120

Art Director: Terry Paulhus Project Coordinator: John Willis

Every reasonable effort has been made to trace ownership and to obtain permission to reprint copyright material. The publisher would be pleased to have any errors or omissions brought to its attention so that they may be corrected in subsequent printings.

The publisher acknowledges Alamy, Getty Images, Minden Pictures, Shutterstock, and Wikimedia as the primary image suppliers for this title.